PRAYING FOR
THE IMPOSSIBLE

PRAYING FOR THE IMPOSSIBLE

by

Buddy Harrison

HARRISON HOUSE

Tulsa, Oklahoma

06   10 9 8 7 6

Praying for the Impossible
ISBN 1-57794-513-1
Copyright © 2002 by Patsy G. Harrison
P.O. Box 35443
Tulsa, Oklahoma 74153

Previously *Petitioning for the Impossible–
The Prayer of Supplication*
(ISBN 0-89274-900-8)
Copyright © 1992 by Buddy Harrison. Revised.

Published by Harrison House, Inc.
P.O. Box 35035
Tulsa, Oklahoma 74153

Contents

1

Overcome the Impossible

Our God is the God of the impossible, but He also expects us to do our part and pray. There are different types of prayer, and they each have guidelines. We must know what to pray for, who to pray for, and how to pray.

The prayer of supplication is the kind of prayer that can be used in critical situations where there seems to be no other way. I have used this prayer during times of crisis in my own life, and they have all been answered within three months.

I don't want to make it sound like this type of prayer will solve every problem that you have, but when our requests line up with God's will, which is simply His Word, then He hears us and He answers.

One time I found myself in a critical situation when, normally, I would have prayed the prayer of faith or the prayer of agreement to bring the answer. At that time, I learned more about another type of prayer that was even more effective for my particular situation.

In February of 1989, the Lord had spoken to my wife, Pat, and me to attend Brother Hagin's Winter Bible Seminar. My publishing company was in the middle of a new thrust in Bibles called topical Bibles. They were making a strong impact in the Christian market. For us to be able to keep a supply of Bibles available, certain things had to happen.

My staff told me we needed a large sum of money, a six digit figure, to complete the project. A few days passed and I hadn't really begun serious prayer about it. The staff told me I had ten days. I said, "Now Lord, I need the finances to buy Bible paper and leather for the covers."

Eventually, I decided to go to the bank and tell them what I needed, but they would only loan me a portion of what I had asked for. The problem was the bank didn't want to give me the money. Part of the money wouldn't produce what I needed. I needed more than the bank's approved loan. In the natural realm there was no way to make this happen.

Usually, I would have depended on Mark 11:24 which says, "What things soever ye desire, when ye pray, believe that ye receive them, and ye shall have them." I didn't have the inner assurance I needed that when I asked I would receive.

When you know the will of God in a particular area, then you can also have faith for it. I knew it was God's will for all men to be saved and these topical Bibles would help to fulfill His will.

It would take more money than what I had, and seven days had already passed. I still didn't have the inner assurance to pray the prayer of faith. I don't know if you have ever used Mark 11:24 and had nothing happen, but I have. Sometimes you can turn your confessor on over-time. "I believe I receive, but Lord, it isn't showing up." Eventually, you fall into a ritual and don't see any results. That wasn't God's fault; it was mine. Time was running out, and I knew I had to find another way.

By now, we were in the middle of the seminar and two of my very close friends, Happy Caldwell and Jerry Savelle, had come to our house. As we talked, I said to them, "Guys, listen. Pray with me about the money I need for these Bibles. Our first shipment has already sold, and I need to move now to keep Bibles in stock for all the orders we have coming in."

There were three days left when I asked my friends to pray with me. I would have prayed the prayer of agreement with them using Matthew 18:19 which says, "if two of you shall agree on earth as touching any thing that they shall ask, it shall be done for them of my Father which is in heaven." I had recently learned more about the application of the prayer of agreement and knew that the prayer of agreement may not be the most effective prayer to use in this situation.

My insight into the prayer of agreement came to me one day after a service. A young man walked up to me and said, "Brother Harrison, does Matthew 18:19 which says, 'if two of you shall agree on earth as touching any thing...' apply to any thing?" Without thinking, the answer came up out of my spirit, "No." It shocked both of us. I was thinking, *Well, what does it mean then?*

My answer was startling to me because I answered him by the Holy Spirit saying, "No, it has to do with any thing *concerning the two of you.* Two people can't agree for Uncle John and Aunt Susy unless their situation also concerns them, but they can intercede for them. This, of course, is a different type of prayer." When I saw this, I realized that I could pray the prayer of agreement *with* people but not *for* them. It changed the way I prayed the prayer of agreement.

The Order of Prayer

If I didn't pray the prayer of faith or the prayer of agreement, I wondered exactly how I should pray. After awhile, Happy spoke up and said, "Buddy, in our intercessory group we have been using the order that is in First Timothy 2, and have been having great success." So, we all turned to First Timothy 2:1 which says, "I exhort therefore, that, first of all, supplications, prayers, intercessions, and giving of thanks, be made for all men."

As we read, Happy began to tell us what he had found. "We're dealing with four types of prayer here, but they're in an order." When Happy pointed out the order, I realized God was trying to teach me. I knew the Holy Spirit was upon him, so I listened closely.

As he talked, I began to see that there were four kinds of prayer and that they were in a particular order: first, supplications; second, prayers; third, intercessions; and fourth, the giving of thanks. Although each of these four types of prayer also work alone, the words, *first of all,* spoke to me of a particular order. God has a certain order that He operates within, and it is our job to understand that order and get in line with it.

Unfortunately, many people's prayer lives are out of order, and they simply don't work. God is a God of order. If you don't understand His order, you mess things up. You need to follow His order so that His blessings can come into your life.

I also noticed that all the prayers mentioned in First Timothy 2 were plural. They could be prayed collectively or individually, and they could be prayed multiple times. Some prayers, like the prayer of faith and the prayer of agreement, you pray one time and that is it. Other prayers, like these, you can pray over and over again.

Although the prayer of faith and the prayer of agreement are very important and powerful prayers, we have almost forgotten about prayers that can be prayed over and over again. I am not criticizing. I am trying to rectify where we have shoved one type of prayer too far. We have overemphasized the prayer of faith and the prayer of agreement and have used them when we should have used other types of prayer.

While Happy continued to teach us what he had found, the Holy Spirit moved on Jerry to say, "We need to pray for the banker and the committee." Then I understood. This prayer in

First Timothy 2 was for *men* (people), not money. The people have the money. God doesn't have any money in heaven. In my situation, the banker was the one who was responsible for the money. He was also the one entrusted with the authority to invest the money.

What the Spirit gave to Jerry came alive inside of me, and we began to pray for the banker so that if he had any committees to answer to, we would have favor with them, and if they had any policy that would keep them from giving us the loan, they would be willing to change it in this instance.

Then Jerry insisted that we write the prayer out. He said it was because the first word, supplication, meant "petition."[1] If we were going to petition the city, the state, or the U. S. government, it would be a formal written request. We decided to write out our prayer in the form of a legal petition. It was about one page in length. Every time we made a statement, we wrote a corresponding

Scripture reference in the margin. Sometimes we included the references within the petition.

As we worked together, we came closer into agreement regarding exactly what we were asking. As we searched the Scriptures to find the promises for what we were asking, my faith was built up and my spirit man became more convinced that what I was asking for was in line with His will for me. After we finished, we prayed through it. Then I knew in my "knower" that our prayer would be manifested.

I was so excited that I called the general manager at my publishing company and said, "Call the bank because they're going to let us have the money." I was excited because I had heard from heaven. I had the witness of the spirit.

The next morning my general manager called the bank. The first thing the banker said was, "We've reviewed the application again, and we can still only loan you a portion of your request." He waited. Then the banker said, "You know we have never allowed you to borrow money against any of your foreign accounts, author's accounts, or C.O.D.'s, but, in this instance, we're going to change our policy." Our supplication had been answered. By borrowing against our accounts and adding it to the portion that they were willing to loan us, we had the money that was necessary for the topical Bibles.

I put into practice what I learned during that week. In a short amount of time I began to see the answers for the petitions that I had made. I developed a greater hunger for the Word, a stronger love for people, and a more intimate relationship with God.

2

Write the Petition Down

I exhort therefore, that, first of all, supplications, prayers, intercessions, and giving of thanks, be made for all men; For kings, and for all that are in authority; that we my lead a quiet and peaceable life in all godliness and honesty.

For this is good and acceptable in the sight of God our Saviour; Who will have all men to be saved, and to come unto the knowledge of the truth. For there is one God, and one mediator between God and men, the man Christ Jesus; Who gave himself a ransom for all, to be testified in due time.

1 Timothy 2:1-6

The prayer of supplication is the first kind of prayer mentioned in this passage and is one of the most powerful prayers in the Word of God because it is so specific and exact. Some prayers are general and produce general answers. In this type of prayer, you can't go by inspiration. You must take time out to put it in writing.

A vision doesn't really become real to you unless you write it down. Habakkuk admonishes us to write the vision down and make it plain so they that read it may run with it. (Hab. 2:2.) Sometimes we lose in the kingdom of God simply because we haven't taken the time to write things down. When we do, we are able to overcome the seemingly impossible.

The progression in prayer First Timothy 2:1 suggests has brought me to the place where I know my prayers are answered when I ask. When I have difficulty discerning the will of God in a matter, when my faith seems low, when I lack inner assurance, or need others to pray in one accord with me about a situation that seems impossible, I find myself using the prayer of supplication.

There are actually three definitions for the word supplication: 1) a petition, 2) an entreaty, or 3) a humble request.[1]

The primary definition for supplications in this verse is "petition" according to *Strongs*.[2] A petition is a "formal written request."[3] It is written in formal terms that deal with the legal side of an issue. It follows acceptable, proper, legal guidelines and is addressed to a person or group in authority. It also requires for some judicial action to be taken.

In First Timothy 2:1, the Greek word for *supplications* is *deesis*. In the New Testament, this supplication is "always addressed to God" as He is the Supreme Authority.[4]

An *entreaty is* "an earnest request." When a request is earnest, it is "1) serious and intense; not joking or playful; zealous and sincere; deeply convinced, 2) intent; fixed, and 3) serious; important; not trivial."[5]

This is a time when you are determined. An intensity is present. The Greek word for supplication used here, *deesis,* "stresses the sense of need" rather than just desire or want.[6]

Passive prayer is communion with God; supplication is intense. James 5:16 talks about the effectual fervent prayer of the righteous man and says that it avails much. Jesus spoke about the days of John the Baptist. "Until now the kingdom of heaven suffereth violence, and the violent take it by force" (Matt. 11:12). Until you become violent with some things, they will never be done. You must make up your mind that you need to have them and that it has to be that way.

There are privileges in boldness that many people don't understand. God tells us to "come boldly unto the throne of grace, that we may obtain mercy, and find grace to help in time of need" (Heb. 4:16). Many do not know the will of God; therefore, when it is time to pray, they play games. God wants you to come seriously, know what His Word says and what you need.

Desperate people in need don't say, "Well, God, if You think it would be all right." When you are faced with a life or death situation, you need to be exact and bold. Walk in and say to the Lord, "You said in Your Word it's this way, and I'm not going to have it any other way." That is not getting smart with God, but puts Him in remembrance of His Word. (Isa. 43:26.)

Often the struggle in prayer is accepting the will of God. Even Jesus struggled with the will of God for His life. "And being in an agony he prayed more earnestly: and his sweat was as it were great drops of blood falling down to the ground" (Luke 22:44). Some things that you pray about can be so hard that a struggle goes on between the spiritual and the natural.

Jesus prayed until the will of His soul was conformed to the will of His Father. He prayed until He could come to that place where He could say "...not my will, but thine, be done" (Luke 22:42). His mind, will, and emotions were brought into subjection to the will of God. We, like Jesus, need to pray until our will is in line with God's will, for only then can we be assured that He will answer.

According to James 4:3, "Ye ask, and receive not, because ye ask amiss, that ye may consume it upon your lusts." When you humble yourself by submitting your will to His will, your prayers will come to pass because you pray His will. Your soul prospers because you submitted your will to His will. Your emotions are under His control. Your mind can be selective in its thought processes, and you can make better choices because they will be made according to the Word of God.

Nearly every letter Paul wrote included his prayers for that church. Although many times he dealt with situations in the church, he also told them he was praying for them. He affected them with his letters because he wrote the supplication down that he was praying for them.

In Ephesians 1:16-19, he ceases not to give thanks for them, making mention of them in his prayers. He asks that the Lord give them the spirit of wisdom and revelation in the knowledge of Him, that the eyes of their understanding be enlightened, that they would know the hope of His calling, the riches of the glory of His inheritance, and the exceeding greatness of His power.

In Ephesians 3:14-19, he bows his knees asking the Lord to strengthen them with might by His Spirit so that Christ can dwell in their hearts by faith, they can be rooted and grounded in love, and be able to comprehend and know the love of Christ. The outcome he asks for is that they be filled with the fullness of God.

In Philippians 1:9-11, he prays that their love will abound in knowledge and judgement so that they will approve things that are excellent and be sincere and without offence till the day of Christ.

In Romans 15:30, he says, "...strive together with me in your prayers to God for me." He asked the churches to join him in prayer. The key phrase here is *strive together* which means "to struggle in the company with."[7] Literally, this word means "to compete for a prize." In a figurative sense, it means "to contend with an adversary."[8] The church was able to strive together with him in prayer more closely because Paul wrote down his prayer. They could come into agreement to a greater degree and be more certain that they were in one accord.

United prayers of this kind can be very powerful. Acts 4:31 records the place which the believers were standing on shook after they had prayed in one accord.

SUPPLICATIONS IN DAVID'S PSALMS

While the supplications in the Epistles deal with the present-day Church and the will of God for our generation, the Psalms also contain a number of supplications. David makes supplication in Psalm 119:170 where he says, "Let my supplication come before thee: deliver me according to thy word." God delivers according to His Word.

In Psalm 28:2, David says, "Hear the voice of my supplications, when I cry unto thee...." In verse 6 he says, "Blessed be the Lord, because he hath heard the voice of my supplications." In verse 7 he goes on to say, "The Lord is my strength and my shield; my heart trusted in him, and I am helped...." That sounds like answered prayer to me.

There is always an assurance of God hearing and answering all our petitions if they are based on the will of God, which is His Word. Psalm 30:8-12 says, "I cried to thee, O Lord; and unto the Lord I made supplication.... Thou hast turned for me my mourning into dancing: thou hast put off my sackcloth, and girded me with gladness; To the end that my glory may sing praise to thee, and not be silent."

God heard David's supplication and answered. God will hear your supplication, and He will answer. He desires to work in your behalf.

Once I began to see what the Scriptures were saying about writing down my requests, I began to teach my staff about it. At that time, the ministry owned a beautiful piece of property on top of a mountain. It had ten wooded acres with two bluffs that dropped two hundred feet into a lake.

The Lord talked to me about selling the property because He planned to use it for ministers, and He wanted us to have property within an hour's drive from the office. This property was five hours away. The staff and I petitioned the Lord about selling the property. I received in my spirit the amount that we should ask for the property. One week later, we had a contract in our hands for $5,000 more than the amount I had received in my spirit. We paid a $5,000 fee to the person who sold it for us, and we received the amount I knew the Lord had told me to expect.

I also began to teach about writing your petition down to people in churches across the nation. One time I preached this in a church in Tucson. An engineer there went to work the very next day and was laid off from his company.

As he was putting up his things he came across his Bible, and the thought hit him that he should present a supplication like I had taught. He took out his Bible, sat down at his desk, searched the Scriptures, and wrote out his petition. Before he had left the building, a man from another division of the company walked in and hired him at a higher rate of pay than he had been making in his previous position. Losing your job can be critical. God didn't want him doing without; instead, he received an increase.

One woman had received phone calls from another woman saying her husband was unfaithful to her. She had seen some signs that what the woman told her may have been true, but she didn't want to believe it. She decided to write out a supplication of protection. She asked that any influences or people that would affect her husband in an adverse way be removed from his life. In just a short period of time, her husband's attitude changed and their relationship became so strong that she was thoroughly confident that he wouldn't be bothered anymore.

Another woman wanted to see her child accepted into a special education program that she felt he needed. The program didn't want to accept him because they felt his situation wasn't severe enough, yet he wasn't receiving the help he needed at a regular school. After hearing me teach, she wrote a supplication addressing her situation. In a couple of weeks, they contacted her and said, "We have an opening, so we'll go ahead and take him."

3

Back Up the Petition

In supplications, you deal with the known will of God. The known will of God is written in His Word. If you will allow the Holy Spirit to lead you and bring to your remembrance Scriptures, you can write your petition under the anointing and unction of the Holy Spirit. If it is in agreement with His Word, you can be sure that it is a part of His will for you.

In Isaiah 43:26, God said, "Put me in remembrance: let us plead together: declare thou, that thou mayest be justified." His Word is His will. When someone writes out his or her will, they are writing a legal document. Your Bible is a legal document and a testimony to what God's will is.

When someone dies, an executor is assigned to carry out the will. He is responsible to make sure that the instructions are followed. Jesus died to make sure God's will would come to pass, and He rose up to watch over it. He is enforcing His own will. What is in that legal document belongs to us.

We are new creations. Old things have passed away, and all things have become new. (2 Cor. 5:17.) We are the head and not the tail. We are above and not beneath. (Deut. 28:13.) All the blessings of God are legally ours.

If you don't know what rightfully belongs to you according to the Word of God, you can never experience all God has provided for you. Your petition establishes, in you and those petitioning with you, the known will of God. This is the legal side of the petition. Once it is established in you, you are in line to experience the will of God in your life. This is the vital side, the practical living side. The legal side must first be established before the vital side can be experienced. If it happens any other way, just chalk it up to God's mercy and grace operating in your behalf.

For example, if you buy a house, you can't enjoy living in it until you have legally completed all the paperwork and paid for it. There is the legal side of having a house, and the vital side of living in it. It is the same with the promises of God. Legally, God's promises are bought, purchased, and paid for, but then there is the vital side, where you actually get a chance to experience His promises in your life. In the church world, we often try to deal with the vital side when we don't yet understand the legal side.

In a court case, you deal with facts, evidence, and proof. The facts of God's Word make the difference. Your faith is your evidence. "Now faith is the substance of things hoped for, the evidence of things not seen" (Heb. 11:1). The Word of God becomes proof to you and to the enemy that you have what you are believing for.

In a supplication you deal with the known will of God, which is the Word of God, and you appeal to the Supreme Court of heaven.

Satan is the head of his kingdom. (2 Cor. 4:4.) He has wicked spirits in high places. He has rulers of the darkness, powers, and principalities. (Eph. 6:12.) He is the accuser of the brethren. (Rev. 12:10.) If you get out of line, he is there to condemn you. If you make one mistake, he can legally take advantage of you. He is a legalist.

God is not a legalist. When you miss it, He is there to restore you. Lamentations 3:22,23 promises that "...his compassions fail not. They are new every morning: great is thy faithfulness." God works for you, not against you. He is the Supreme Judge of the universe. When you make your appeal to Him, you address the Supreme Court of heaven.

God is the Most High God. There isn't anyone higher than He is. When you use His Word in His court, you win. When you know that, you are bold. It is not hit and miss. There is a way to pray in absolute confidence so that there are no questions nor doubts that you have the answer.

You have an Advocate—Jesus. (1 John 2:1.) He is the Lawyer who pleads your case. Whatever words you say to Him, He uses to plead your case. If you use His Words to plead your case in His Father's court, the outcome is sure. The case is fixed.

You have the Holy Spirit who is the sheriff. A judge can decree a thing and pass judgement on it, but there must be an enforcer. The Holy Spirit makes sure God's Word is carried out on the earth. The angels also do their part.

In Acts 4, Peter and John preached to the people, and the priests seized them and put them in prison overnight. When the priests released them the next day, they returned to their own company.

After they told them what had happened, everyone "lifted up their voice to God with one accord" (Acts 4:24). You come into one accord when everyone says the same thing. One sure way to get everyone to say the same thing is to write down the request. It seems that even the early church must have written down their request. It is written in the Scripture.

Their request seems to follow the form of a petition. They begin in Acts 4:24 by listing the Scriptures relative to their situation. First, they go to Genesis and magnify the God of all creation. They remind Him and themselves that He created the heaven, the earth, the sea, and all that are in them. Then they go to the Psalms and quote the words of David from Psalm 2:1,2 which speak of the rejection of the Messiah and His anointed.

In verses 26 and 27, they identify four classes of people that came against Christ: the kings of the earth, the rulers of Israel; the heathen Gentiles, and the people of Israel. In verse 29, they ask the Lord to behold the threats that are being hurled against them by these same people.

After identifying the Scriptures that applied to their situation, they made their request and asked for boldness to speak His Word and for signs and wonders to be done by the name of Jesus. Their request was in line with God's will which is to go into all the world and preach the gospel to every creature. (Mark 16:15.) They had completed the legal side of their request. Now they were ready to experience the vital side.

They didn't have to wait long because in verse 31, their first request is answered when the place where they stood was shaken; they were all filled with the Holy Spirit and began to speak the Word with boldness. Their second request was answered shortly thereafter when they hit the streets. Acts 5:12 records that many signs and wonders were wrought among the people by the hands of the apostles.

The supplication was answered; one part instantly and the other later. God is always ready to answer your supplications because He lives in the eternal now. God is the great I am. (Ex. 3:14.) *Am* is in the present tense. He is ready to do it now, so when you pray, believe that the promises of God are yea and amen in Christ Jesus. (2 Cor. 1:20.)

A PERSONAL PETITION

Write down your own petition to God. You can't copy another person's supplication. You have to dig into the Word of God and write your own. You need to know why you said what you said, and it needs to be real to you. The Holy Spirit will lead and guide you into all truth. You may also want to thumb through the Epistles, Psalms, and Proverbs. As you read the Word of God and study, you will find Scriptures that you know will fit your petition. Mark and write them down so you will have them to refer to when you begin.

The only caution I might add is that you not include in your petition any dates. I did this a couple of times and hadn't received an answer to them for quite a few months. My spirit stayed slightly grieved, but I couldn't understand why. The Lord said, "Go back and look at your petitions." So I went back and looked, and He said, "You know why they weren't answered and why you were frustrated in your spirit? It was because you wrote dates in it. You can have goals without dates."

I was reminded then of Mark 11:24 which says, "What things soever ye desire, *when ye pray, believe that ye receive* them, and ye shall have them." The emphasis is on believing that you receive *when you pray.* Except for those two petitions that I added dates to, they have all been answered within one to ninety days.

As you write your petition, you may want to refer to the one that I wrote below. Write yours out however works best for you.

PETITIONER'S ORIGINAL REQUEST

Eph. 6:17,18	This petition is being brought to God because of His Word. It is being
Rom. 13:1	brought to the Highest Authority in the universe over the Supreme Court.
1 John 2:1,2	I am represented by Jesus Christ, my Advocate. There has been a change of rep-
Col. 1:13	resentation by counsel, and Satan no longer represents

me because he is not my lord or lawyer any longer.

Ps. 100:4
Ps. 116:1,2
Ps. 136
Ps. 118:1-6
Ps. 105:5-8
Ps. 18:1-6

I am thankful that I can petition this court, for God has done great things for me. My account has been identified by the written Word, and again I want to give thanks. All relief for petitioners was granted in full.

The basis for grant of relief in contract is established by the Old Covenant with Abraham, because He could

Heb. 6:13

swear by no greater, He sware by Himself. But I have a better covenant

Heb. 8:6
Gal. 3:29
Gal. 3:13,14

established upon better promises. I became an heir, through my Agent, Jesus,

Col. 2:13,14
Heb. 9:15

when He sealed it by His blood for a new covenant.

Write in the verses that apply to your specific requests in the column below.

Therefore, I have every right to be here and have the relief sought, and You, God, have the authority to issue a decree in this matter.

So I request to be granted the following specific request for relief:

_____

_____

_____

1. _____

_____

2. _____

_____

3. _____

_____

John 10:10

For Satan has come as a thief to steal, kill and to destroy, but Your promise

Ps. 119:170

to me was in Your Word and by Your Spirit which You gave me. This is the petitioner's prayer, and I am asking for a summary judgement.

Ps. 4:6-8
1 John 5:14,15

I cast all of my care on You, for I know You have heard me, and I have it.

So therefore, it is ordered, adjudged, and decreed that the petitioner receive that relief sought in this petition immediately according to Mark 11:23,24.

Ps. 103:20

Be it further ordered, adjudged, and decreed that the agents of God implement such findings immediately pursuant to the Word. In other words,

Holy Spirit and angels, do God's Word.

Again, let me say thank You for all You have done and are doing now. I know You shall continue to bless all who see and serve You.

DATED THIS THE _____ DAY OF _____, 20____.

PETITIONERS:

_____   _____

(name)   (name)

_____   _____

(name)   (name)

_____   _____

(name)   (name)

ANSWERED THIS THE_____ DAY OF _____, 20____.

ESTABLISH THE KNOWN WILL OF GOD

This petition is simply a pattern to declare your rights and privileges. When you write your petitions based upon the Word of God, you establish the known will of God. When you pray it aloud, you build up your faith in what you already know, for "faith cometh by hearing, and hearing by the word of God" (Rom. 10:17). Faith is essential to prayer, for faith is the recognition and the committal of yourself and your matters to the faithfulness of God. When you are established in the known will of God, you can ask in faith with nothing wavering so that you can receive from the Lord what He has already promised you. (James 1:5-8.)

When you pray your petition, you should pray it as a present possession, as if you already possess it. Hebrews 11:1 says that faith is in the now, not in the past or the future. It is in the present. There is a certainty to it. If time passes and the petition that you made doesn't feel like you have it, go back and read it again until it gets down on the inside of you so that you know that you know. For "without faith it is impossible to please him" (Heb. 11:6).

4

Pray the Petition Through

The Word says in First John 5:14,15, "...if we ask any thing according to his will, he heareth us: And if we know that he hear us, whatsoever we ask, we know that we have the petitions that we desired of him." According to this verse, we must first *ask* according to His will, and secondly, we must *know* that He hears us.

Both the Word of God and prayer are mentioned when Paul talks to the church in Ephesus about spiritual warfare. In Ephesians, chapter six, Paul expounds on the armor of God:

Wherefore take unto you the whole armour of God, that ye may be able to withstand in the

evil day, and having done all, to stand. Stand therefore, having your loins girt about with truth, and having on the breastplate of righteousness; And your feet shod with the preparation of the gospel of peace;

Above all, taking the shield of faith, wherewith ye shall be able to quench all the fiery darts of the wicked. And take the helmet of salvation, and the sword of the Spirit, which is the word of God: Praying always with all prayer and supplication in the Spirit, and watching thereunto with all perseverance and supplication for all saints.

Ephesians 6:13-18

When Paul lists the armor, he talks about the defensive and the offensive types of armor. The Word of God and prayer are the only two pieces of the armor that are offensive while all the other pieces are defensive. It is when we are on the offensive with the enemy that we can do more than hold our ground. When we take an offensive position, we can actually claim what rightfully

belongs to us. That is what the prayer of supplication does.

Most of the time, we think about the sword of the Spirit in our hand, but it is really in our mouths. When Paul wrote to the church, he wrote a letter. When you write a letter, you don't break it up and number it. The numbers were added to Paul's letter so we could reference what he said and refer to them for study purposes, but the original letters weren't divided up.

If we read Ephesians 6:17,18, forgetting the punctuation and the numbering in an effort to bring back the original flow of the language, it would read, *Take the helmet of salvation and the sword of the Spirit which is the word of God praying.* This emphasizes that the sword of the Spirit is the Word of God praying. Jesus is the Word. Jesus knows how to pray, and He is powerful.

If, in turn, I use the equipment God has given me, the Word of God praying, His Words become my words. I take His Word and pray it. Isaiah 55:11 says, "So shall my word be that goeth forth out of my mouth: it shall not return unto me void, but it shall accomplish that which I please, and it shall prosper in the thing whereto I sent it."

Notice also that it is the Word of God "praying always with all prayer" (Eph. 6:18). *The Amplified* translation of this verse says, "with all [manner of] prayer." Where we have made a mistake much of the time is that we have used the wrong prayer in the wrong situation. We have lacked knowledge in some areas, and God wants to expand our knowledge because knowledge is a vital part in living the victorious life.

Going further in verse 18, Paul says, "Praying always with all prayer and supplication in the Spirit, and watching thereunto with all persever-ance and supplication for all saints." It is supplica-tion *in the Spirit for all saints.* We should pray for our brothers and sisters in the Lord and for one another. It is a part of the armor of God. The armor is more than just praying in the Holy Spirit. It is also praying the Word of God. It is literally Jesus' Word being prayed out.

You have the sword of the Spirit coming out of your mouth which is the Word of God praying. It is so powerful and dynamic because you pray His own Word which is full of life eternal. (Isa. 40:8.) For Him to deny His Word, He has to deny Himself. God can't deny Himself. (2 Tim. 2:13.) He is who He is, and His Word has said so. Therefore, it shall be so.

A supplication can be prayed more than once. Every time the situation seems like it isn't lining up with my petition, I take out the supplication and pray it again. This produces faith in me and brings me an assurance; therefore, I am stable and unwavering. I pray it until I am established in it. Sooner or later, it has to come to pass. Most of the time, it is sooner rather than later.

The church prayed without ceasing. (Acts 12:5-17.) Peter was to die. (Acts 12:1-4.) The church prayed using the armor of God. They began in the morning and continued into the night. God was at work, but they didn't know it yet.

Verse 5 says, "Peter therefore was kept in prison: but prayer was made without ceasing of the church unto God for him." *Without ceasing* literally means "stretched out" which "signifies earnest, fervent."[1]

A person or animal is stretched out intensely the closer they get to the finish line when running a race. They earnestly and fervently try to make it to the other side.

In supplications in the Spirit, the Holy Spirit begins to take over. Although you may not pray in tongues, you pray by the power of the Spirit of God. (Rom. 8:26,27.) You will find yourself stretching out to grab it, take hold of it, and lock on to it.

The church was down to serious business because Peter was in trouble. This wasn't a passive prayer but an active prayer. It was a prayer that brought supernatural deliverance to Peter while he was still in chains. That very night while Peter was sleeping, an angel of the Lord came to him in the prison and said, "...Arise up quickly" (Acts 12:7).

The chains fell from Peter's hands, and he followed the angel out of the prison, through the gate, and out onto the streets. Soon after, the angel departed from him, and he ran back to the group that had been praying for *him* without ceasing. Their instant and earnest supplication for him throughout the night had literally saved his life.

The church had made their request according to God's will. They had met the first condition mentioned in First John 5:14,15. They also met the second condition, which is to know that He hears us. They continued in prayer until they knew that they knew.

I have found that the progression in prayer that First Timothy 2:1 suggests has brought me to that place of knowing. Once I know, nothing and no one can stop me from receiving the petitions that I desire of Him. His Word and the witness of His Spirit with my spirit make me certain it is already mine, and He won't deny His Word.

The second kind of prayer mentioned in First Timothy 2, is often linked with supplication in other passages of Scripture. (Acts 1:14; Eph. 6:18; Phil. 4:6; 1 Tim. 5:5.) *Prayers,* in First Timothy 2:1, means "worship."[2]

Spiritual worship, rather than mental or physical worship, is actually a form of prayer. In John 4:24, it says, "God is a Spirit: and they that worship him must worship him in spirit and in truth." As a spirit being, you worship a Spirit Being, so everything has to begin at that point.

The raising of hands, for example, may be worship, and it may not.

Are you thinking about the roast in the oven at home for dinner? That is not worship but just raising your hands. If you focus on God as the object of your worship and become more conscious of Him while raising your hands, then you are really worshipping.

The Holy Spirit helps you in your worship. Your spirit is the part of you that motivates you to worship. Your mind and your body simply fall in line with your spirit.

You start with supplications which deal with the known will of God. You use your mind to write down your supplication because it has to do with what you know. Then you begin to worship. Worship is the hookup that takes you from the mental realm into the spiritual realm of intercession. You move from one dimension into another—out of the natural, logical, mental realm and into the spiritual realm as you worship.

First, you worship with your understanding, then, as the Spirit leads you, you worship using the language of the spirit, which is tongues. One is in a known language while the other is in an unknown language.

As you worship or pray in an unknown language, the Holy Spirit will begin to intercede through you for the things you don't know about. According to Paul in Romans "...we know not what we should pray for as we ought: but the Spirit itself maketh intercession for us with groanings which cannot be uttered" (Rom. 8:26). Paul is talking about the Holy Spirit. Jesus referred to Him as "another Comforter" in John 14:16.

Comforter in the Greek literally means "called to one's side."[3] Historically, the word *comforter* "was used in a court of justice to denote a legal assistant, counsel for the defence, an advocate;

then, generally, one who pleads another's cause, an intercessor, advocate."[4] The word *another* implies they are of the same sort rather than a different sort.[5] The Holy Spirit and Jesus are made of the same substance, and they work together along side us in the heavenly court of justice.

At some point while I am praying in tongues, the Holy Spirit begins to intercede through me. The word, *intercessions,* as it is used in First Timothy 2:1, means "seeking the presence and hearing of God on behalf of others."[6] At one time, it was "a technical term for approaching a king, and so for approaching God in intercession."[7]

The Holy Spirit comes along side of you and helps you to pray. Because He is a part of the Godhead, He knows all things and is able to pray for things that you don't even know about. He will not pray anything against the will of God. He can only pray the will of God. When you finish, you

53

know that you have prayed the perfect prayer and have covered all the bases.

Whenever I have finished interceding, I know that I know. If I don't reach that place, I go back and worship God again. Usually, I receive an utterance in tongues and interpret it. Through the interpretation, God tells me what I have to do next so that I am never in the dark. I either know I have it, or I know what to do next. It gets rid of those "Well let's pray and leave it up to God" prayers.

In First Corinthians 14:15, Paul mentions a similar approach, "I will pray with the spirit, and I will pray with the understanding also: I will sing with the spirit, and I will sing with the under-standing also." By beginning with supplications then moving into worship and intercessions, prayer is taken out of the mystical realm and put into the spiritual order of God so that it can work.

GIVING OF THANKS

A natural response following the prayer of supplication, spiritual worship, and intercession is the giving of thanks. In the giving of thanks, we express gratitude. Surely if we ask someone for something and they promise to give it to us, common courtesy would say, "Thank you." When you ask God for something He has promised you in His Word, you shouldn't have to be told to say, "Thank you." Yet many petitions are not complete simply because they lack a word of thanks.

Today, we live in an instant society, and we want to approach God on that instant basis. Then we wonder why it isn't working too well. Anything worthwhile takes time. If you are going to have a good marriage, it is going to take time. If you are going to have a good church, it is going to take time.

You might say, "But God, I asked You. How come I don't have it?" You may have a bad attitude. You may not have a thankful heart. You need to be kind and gracious. He saved you. He healed you. He filled you with His Spirit. You have so many things to be thankful for. Those two words, as small as they are, can make all the difference.

Psalm 118:1-29 is a biblical example of what I call the sandwich theory, which places the request in the middle of the prayer and thanksgiving at the beginning and the end. David spends the first twenty-four verses of his petition giving thanks to God because: He is good, His mercy endures forever, He answers when David calls on Him, He puts him in a large place, He is on David's side, He takes his part, He is his strength, song, and salvation, and finally, just because He has heard him. It is interesting to notice here that his petition is only one verse long: "Save now, I beseech thee, O Lord: O Lord, I beseech thee, send now prosperity" (v. 25). Then after he has made his request, he goes back to thanking and praising God in the last four verses. David was a man after God's own heart who prospered. David was more conscious of giving thanks unto God than of his need.

In the story of the ten lepers found in Luke 17:12-19, the lepers were healed and cleansed, but only one was made whole. He was a Samaritan, not a Jew. He had returned to thank and praise Jesus for what He had done. Jesus told him that his faith had made him whole.

The skin of lepers often rotted off. Many times they lost members of their body. All ten were healed and cleansed, but the leper who returned to thank and praise Him also had his members restored. God will honor faith, and healing will come. An attitude of gratitude will make you whole. That which is missing will be replaced.

For some time, I wanted my son to be able to obtain a different car. He had a sports car, lived in an apartment, and was endeavoring to go to school. He couldn't handle the more expensive car. He needed a more economical car, but you know how twenty-year-olds are. The economical part isn't so important. What he needed was a car that was economical *and* looked good.

I petitioned the Lord concerning a car for him. I listed all that was important to my son and to me. I petitioned the Lord on Saturday. On the way home after church Sunday night, I bought a newspaper. I went through the paper marking the cars that looked interesting to me.

I got up praying the next morning, praising and thanking God for His leading me to do the right thing. My eyes were drawn to one particular car, so I called the owner. The car sounded like it would be a good deal. I drove out and saw it. It looked good. I called my son and had him meet me. He saw it and liked it. By 11:00 A.M. we had found and bought a car. All we had to do was let our request be made known to God and begin thanking Him for it.

The verses following First Timothy 2:1 tell you exactly who you should pray for, "For kings, and for all that are in authority" (1 Tim. 2:2). You may have a tendency to take this verse of Scripture and pray for the president. I know I did. We thought we were praying for those in authority, so we prayed for the king, prime minister, judges, supreme court, or someone in a high position.

Look again at verses 1 and 2. He says, "I exhort therefore, that, first of all, supplications, prayers, intercessions, and giving of thanks, be made for all men; For kings, and for all that are in authority." The first verse emphasizes, *for all men,* while the second verse says, *for kings.* God has made all believers kings according to Revelations 1:6. This Scripture also applies to the believer. Ephesians 6:18 emphasizes the believer when referring to prayer and supplication. The only difference is that this verse uses the phrase *...for all saints.*

The second part of verse 2 says, "for all that are in authority." According to W. E. Vine, a marginal note in the *Authorized Version* defines "authority" as an "eminent place."[8]

A cab driver can hold an eminent place within his realm of authority—the cab and the people in the cab. Too many times, we have taken this Scripture and applied it only to a small group of people when God meant for it to apply to a much larger group of people.

It applies not only to those in a place of high authority but also to those with an eminent place, an important place. Whether you know it or not, ushers have an eminent place in the church. They have authority. Their pastors gave it to them.

Let me give you an illustration. My staff and I were scheduled to go on a retreat. At this particular hotel the meals had never been very good. When the secretary set it up, they wanted to serve cokes and coffee when we arrived. She told them not to do that and asked that they serve them after dinner. Well, they didn't pay any attention to her instructions.

We checked into the hotel in the afternoon and were relaxing. When it was almost time to eat, we cleaned up and went to the meeting room. I walked in and there was no meal. There was only one waiter in the hotel, and he was doing room service.

My first thought was, *I'm paying the bill here. I will see that they straighten this out. If I don't get satisfaction with the catering people, I'm going to the manager. If he doesn't like it, I'll go to the owner of this place. If I have to, I'll go to the headquarters that runs this chain.*

Now, there are times when we have rights. I am one of those people who tries to be sweet, but some people are just sweet by nature. My wife is one of those sweet people. I have to work at it. I am a mover and a shaker. If it doesn't look like it will work, I will make it work.

Many times as Christians we have misunderstood our rights and have rolled over and played dead when we should have stood up. Then there are times when we stood up that we should have laid down. It takes wisdom to know when to do what. Right then, I was on my high horse and was ready to straighten someone out.

The Spirit of the Lord said, "Why don't you practice what you preach?" Immediately, I began to follow the order of prayer I had learned.

Our people are free and easy, so they were serving themselves the coffee and water. Those were the only items in the room. Now remember, the waiter is doing room service too. He was all uptight and came running in saying, "If you'll put that down, I'll wait on you. Just wait." He was all bent out of shape and frustrated. We were trying to have something to drink while we waited. The tension was building in him.

The Spirit of the Lord said to me, "Befriend the waiter." So I began to cut up with him and made him laugh. I prayed for the catering man, the cook, and waiter. I prayed for these men because they were the ones with the food. The catering man had the authority. He was the one who said to fix the food.

I could have stood there and said, "Father, I thank You that according to Mark 11:24, I believe I receive my food." I could have kept confessing and confessing, but I would have been misapplying the Scripture. When we do that, we can become mad at God because He hasn't answered our prayer.

In this instance, I needed to pray for men. When I prayed for men, the food was served faster than any time I could remember, and it was the best we had ever had there. It startled me.

Jesus died for people, yet many times we spend all our time praying for things. I am not against praying for things, but why not spend our time praying for the people who have the authority over those things?

The result of praying according to the order of First Timothy 2:1 can be found in verse 2 "...a quiet and peaceable life." Do you want to live a quiet and peaceable life? Things would not have been quiet and peaceable at the hotel if I had raised my voice and demanded my rights. When I prayed according to First Timothy 2:1, I had a quiet and peaceable life.

After I had befriended the waiter, I went up to him at the end of the meal and put my arm around him and said, "You sure have been a blessing to us. I want to pray with you." He said, "No, I have to do room service, so I have to go." He was nervous. The next day when I saw him, he said, "Hey, how are you, Mr. Harrison?" He was open to me, and I could witness to him. If I had demanded my rights the night before, I couldn't have witnessed to him.

Look at verses 3 and 4: "For this is good and acceptable in the sight of God our Saviour; Who will have all men to be saved." When we live a quiet and peaceable life, it is easier for us to reach out to others and for them to receive what we have. He wants them saved from the wrath of men, saved from sin, and saved from circumstances. "For there is one God, and one mediator between God and men, the man Christ Jesus; Who gave himself a ransom for all, to be testified in due time" (1 Tim. 2:5,6).

Just as the healing process can be sped up, so can people's salvation. When everything is kept right, the wound is cleaned out and bandaged properly, it can heal more quickly because it doesn't have to fight infection. So it is with people's salvation. When they haven't been abused and battered by Christians, their due time can come sooner.

Many times God has to work around His people and the damaging words they have spoken. They get out there and make such a mess. It would help them if they would slow down and pray for people.

Many times Brother Hagin has said, "It's better to be too slow than too fast." I went to the Lord to find the truth in what Brother Hagin was saying. I wanted to understand. The Lord said, "It's better to be too slow than too fast because it's easier to play catch up than clean up." That is why many people aren't in the kingdom today. Some Christians are too quick with their temper. They say the wrong thing to people and make such a mess. Sometimes it takes someone else to come in and love the people until they reach the due time of their salvation.

I am not criticizing, but I do think we have lacked knowledge and haven't done things in order. If we will put it in order, it will work. It will be pleasing to God and will speed up people's salvation.

There have been times when my personal life and ministry have come under attack for things from the past. The past is the past. It is over. Spiritual sheriffs want to clean everything up and straighten everyone out. I have news for them. Only the blood of Jesus can do that.

When I came under attack, my first thought was, *God, strike him dead.* Immediately inside, I knew I didn't get that from God because God is a God of love. He said, "...Vengeance is mine; I will repay" (Rom. 12:19).

My job is to pray for them. Jesus, in His Sermon on the Mount, admonishes us to pray for those who despitefully use us and persecute us. (Matt. 5:44.) So I did. I took off time to pray and fast and find the Scriptures that dealt with this particular situation.

In the meantime, I was mutilated, butchered, and crucified. It is hard to keep your mouth shut and pray the most effective prayer. I wouldn't pray in rage and anger. Fear tried to flood me. I thought *I won't be able to preach again.* But I searched the Scriptures, stayed in the Word, and prayed in the Holy Spirit.

My ministry was under attack because of my past. People were saying things. Fear tried to grip me and say that my ministry would be destroyed, and I would never amount to anything. Fear said, "This is the end. Call it quits."

It took ten days of fasting and prayer before I could have the heart and mind of Christ. It took me that long to get myself purged and cleansed. I wrote a petition. This was the first time I had written out a petition in the area of relationships. I had petitioned the Lord in some less critical situations, but this was the first time I was dealing with something that was damaging to my heart, mind, and ministry.

After considering wise counsel, I wrote out my supplication and made it as legal as I could. My supplication was a little over two pages. Every time I made a statement, I wrote the Scripture reference in the margin. Out to the side, I had thirty-four Scripture references, plus eight in the supplication. So, I had forty-two references in all.

At the end of ten days, I had a prayer that I could pray. I prayed that prayer for that individual and two other people. One week later, all the evil communication from these three had dried up. The storm blew over because God won't deny His Word. Prayer is the better way.

The normal reaction is to talk about them, fight, argue, and criticize. The Church has resorted to the world's ways for years. God is ready to bring us in line with His truth and have us praying for those who would despitefully use us and speak evil of us. (Matt. 5:44.) In the process, we start to love them and have nothing but the utmost respect and esteem for them.

Only God can put that in you. You can't manufacture it on your own no matter how good it may sound. When it isn't there, it isn't there. If God doesn't create the love inside of you by His Word and Spirit, it is all vanity and your efforts are futile.

I walk in freedom because I am in love with them. I don't have anything bad to say about them. I have nothing but good words to speak. I am praying for them, and the situation has turned around. It died a quick death because I prayed the truth of God's Word. It is nothing I have done. It is not because I am a greater individual. It is all in God, in His Word, in His Spirit, and by the power of His name. I can be on top and shout the victory. I have no condemnation. I can go on and affect the lives God wants me to affect.

KNOWING HIM

The Bible says you will know the truth, and the truth will make you free. (John 8:32.) It is knowing the truth that makes you free. Jesus makes you free, but this doesn't become a reality until you know Him.

Everybody has their own working relationship with God. And you can't box anyone in. The key to what makes it real and valuable is if you will build that intimacy with God so you know Him. When you know His voice, you don't have to have the spectacular. Let Him speak to you in the way that He always does.

The only way you will get to know His voice is to spend time with Him and develop an intimate relationship. Take my wife and me, for example. I can be in Botswana, Australia, or Japan, but when I call my wife, she knows my voice. She has heard it enough times that she knows who I am without me even telling her my name.

Most Christians know the voice of the flesh and the voice of fear. There are many voices out there, and they all have significance. The real question is, do you know His voice? Do you know Him?

To some people, God is way up in the heavens. That is wonderful and magnificent, but He also happens to be right down here standing right beside me. He is my friend, and I have Him in my heart with my arms wrapped around Him.

You may be questioning me right now feeling overwhelmed by your problems and circum-stances. You may be saying, "I can't do anything right. My life is a mess, and it will always be that way." But that is a lie out of the pit of hell, for with God, all things are possible, but you have to get into the Word and spend some time with your Heavenly Father. As you do this, He will minister to you.

Maybe you find yourself in one of those criti-cal situations where there seems to be no way out, then the prayer of supplication is what you need to pray. First, sit down and write out your petition. Then search the Scriptures to make sure that your request is in line with His will for you. Include those Scriptures in your petition. As you do this, you will find that your faith is rising. Your hope will turn to faith as you come to know what God's Word has to say about your situation.

Your supplication has dealt with the known will of God. But since your knowledge is limited, you must give the Holy Spirit free reign to deal with the unknown elements that may be involved. To do this, you must pray in your prayer language using the prayer of intercession. Worship is one of the best ways that you can make the transition from the mental realm to the spiritual realm. As you have your mind and your heart focused on Him, He will begin to take a hold together with you as you pray. Your prayer will be according to the will of your Heavenly Father and will cover all that you didn't know to pray. When you finish, you will have prayed according to all that you knew and covered every base that you didn't know. You will know that you know that you know. No one and no circumstance will be able to persuade you otherwise.

When you finish, it will be easy to thank Him because you will know that you have the petition that you desired of Him, and in the process you will have come to know Him and His love for you in a greater measure. When you pray like this, you can't be defeated, and you will see situations that you thought were impossible become possible with God.

A Psalm of Praise

So lift up your countenance and rejoice with me in the psalm that the Lord has given me saying:

I'm so glad I'm free.
Satan has no hold on me

'cause I'm free, and I'm rejoicing ever more.
Bless God, I've walked through a brand new
    spiritual door,
a door of prayer, and a door of praise.
And I'm gonna' do it with my hands upraised
'cause the Spirit of God, He's quickening me.
He's flowing mightily and flowing free.

So I'm rejoicing, and I'm singing the song.
I'm gonna' do it all the day long
'cause the power of God is coming alive.
Yes, sir, I'm gonna' jive.
Some of you have been confused.
You've thought, *By the world, I've been used.*
How can I arise and sing?
I need the help of my glorious King.

Well, arise and stand in this hour,
and He'll deliver you by His power.
As you begin to praise,
it will not be delayed

'cause the Spirit of God wants to work in you.

He wants to work in every one of you.

So allow His power to arise so strong,

and you'll find the days will no longer be real
dreadful and long.

But you'll arise with a freshness of heart,

and you'll realize then that the Spirit of God is
not going to depart.

But He'll sustain you and keep you by His
power

because you're about to enter into your finest
hour,

the finest hour for the Church to sing,

the finest hour to worship the King,

the finest hour to overcome,

the finest hour because the victory is already
won.

So rejoice and sing a brand new song

and do it all the day long.

Endnotes

Chapter 1

[1] James Strong, *The Exhaustive Concordance of the Bible* (McLean: MacDonald Publishing, 1978), "Greek Dictionary of the New Testament," p. 21, #1162.

Chapter 2

[1] *Webster's New Twentieth Century Dictionary,* 2nd ed., s.v. "supplication."

[2] Strong, p. 21, #1162.

[3] *Webster's,* s.v. "petition."

[4] W. E. Vine, *An Expository Dictionary of New Testament Words* (Old Tappan: Fleming H. Revell, 1966), Vol. III, p. 200, s.v. "PRAY, PRAYER," "B. Nouns," No. 3 *deesis.*

[5] Webster's, s.v. "earnest."

[6] Vine, Vol. III, p. 200, No. 4, "notes," (I).

[7] Strong, p. 68, #4865.

[8] Strong, p. 8, #75.

Chapter 4

[1] Vine, p. 177, s.v. "CEASE," "C. adverb."

[2] Strong, p. 61, #4335.

[3] Vine, p. 208, s.v. "COMFORT, COMFORTER, COMFORTLESS," "A. Nouns," No. 5.

[4] Vine, p. 208.

[5] Vine, see p. 60, s.v. "ANOTHER."

[6] Vine, Vol. II, p. 267, s.v. "INTERCESSIONS," "A. Noun."

[7] Vine, Vol. II, p. 267.

[8] Vine, p. 89, s.v. "AUTHORITY," "A. nouns," No. 1.

About the Author

DR. DOYLE "BUDDY" HARRISON

"By discipline and training you will receive more; and by being faithful and obedient, God will impart even more, so that you can fulfill the Leadership position God has called you to."

—Buddy Harrison

Buddy Harrison, along with his wife, Pat, were Co-Founders of Faith Christian Fellowship International Church. He served as President of the organization from 1978 until he went home to be with the Lord on November 28, 1998. The Lord instructed Buddy to be a Pastor to Pastors and Ministers, providing guidance for them in the spiritual and natural realms. FCF International is in relationship with more than 1000 churches and 2000 ministers globally. Its programs include: Credentialing for ministers, Affiliation and Association of Churches, Strategic Planning, Family Care Center, Legal Advice, Accounting Consultation, On-site Management consultation,

Stewardship Services, and International Missions Program. It partners with The Life Link for humanitarian outreach. Dr. Harrison strongly believed in the value of covenant relationships and walking under authority, and he set the example for the FCF family. Today, under the leadership of Pat Harrison, FCF continues to foster solid covenant relationships around the world among its ministers and churches.

As the Co-Founder and Chairman of Harrison House Publishers, Buddy obeyed God's vision to provide ministers a vehicle by which to put their message into print.

Harrison House continues to publish timely biblical messages for the body of Christ, fulfilling their mission to challenge Christians to live victoriously, grow spiritually, and know God intimately.

Buddy Harrison successfully incorporated his knowledge and skills of the corporate world with the Lord's calling on his life. As an anointed teacher and astute businessman, he traveled the world sharing these steps-to-success and favor.

To contact Mrs. Pat Harrison

write:

Faith Christian Fellowship International Church, Inc.

P. O. Box 35443

Tulsa, OK 74153-0443

918-492-5800

web site: www.fcf.org

Please include your prayer requests

and comments when you write.

Other Books by Buddy Harrison

God's Banking System

Four Keys to Power

Getting in Position to Receive

How to Raise Your Kids in Troubled Times

Just Do It

Maintaining a Spirit-Filled Life

Man, Husband, Father

Seven Steps to a Quality Decision

The Force of Mercy
(co-authored by Dr. Michael Landsman)

Understanding Authority for Effective Leadership

Understanding Spiritual Gifts

Prayer of Salvation

God loves you—no matter who you are, no matter what your past. God loves you so much that He gave His one and only begotten Son for you. The Bible tells us that "...whoever believes in him shall not perish but have eternal life" (John 3:16 NIV). Jesus laid down His life and rose again so that we could spend eternity with Him in heaven and experience His absolute best on earth. If you would like to receive Jesus into your life, say the following prayer out loud and mean it from your heart.

Heavenly Father, I come to You admitting that I am a sinner. Right now, I choose to turn away from sin, and I ask You to cleanse me of all unrighteousness. I believe that Your Son, Jesus, died on the cross to take away my sins. I also believe that He rose again from the dead so that I might be forgiven of my sins and made righteous through faith in Him. I call upon the name of Jesus Christ to be the Savior and Lord of my life. Jesus, I choose to follow You and ask that You fill me with the power of the Holy Spirit. I declare that right now I am a child of God. I am free from sin and full of the righteousness of God. I am saved in Jesus' name. Amen.

If you prayed this prayer to receive Jesus Christ as your Savior for the first time, please contact us on the web at www.harrisonhouse.com to receive a free book.

Or you may write to us at
Harrison House
P.O. Box 35035
Tulsa, Oklahoma 74153

Additional copies of this book

are available from your local bookstore.

HARRISON HOUSE

Tulsa, Oklahoma 74153

The Harrison House Vision

Proclaiming the truth and the power

Of the Gospel of Jesus Christ

With excellence;

Challenging Christians to

Live victoriously,

Grow spiritually,

Know God intimately.